Who Moved My B●●bs?

Isabelle Tolling

Pierce Publishing
Greenville, South Carolina

First Printing June 2011

Copyright © 2011 by Isabelle Tolling

ISBN: 978-0-9837103-0-1

Library of Congress Control Number: 2011909518

Printed in the United States of America
Set in Palatino Linotype
Edited by Amanda L. Capps
Book Design by Michael Seymour
Cover Design by Alix Cloud

Dedicated to Tom and Ray

Table of Contents

Food is my Friend

We ate until we almost burst
Steaks and chops and liverwurst
I love to eat the fattening stuff
I can't imagine the term *enough*

I love mashed potatoes and Swiss fondue
Maybe even more than you
The world of breads and Direct TV
Is all that waits for me

Okay I'll stop, I know it's not my soul I feel
When the sushi and chocolate bars congeal
If my body hates it, it should rebel
Oh, yours did? Really, do tell

The doctor has restricted your diet
Tell me later, there's a buffet at the Hyatt

Plane Travel

I know that smell of planes too old
When filth has seeped into every fold
When bathroom smell reeks to my seat
And turbulence makes our trip complete
I know the "SkyMall" magazine by heart
And when the in-aisle briefing soon will start
I know the 20-somethings who won't stop texting
Or when the flight attendant is mad or vexing
You cannot go pee when the cart is present
You'd think they were serving foie gras or pheasant

When I was a child, we flew on the Pan Am Clipper
With linen real silver and sleeper berths in it
It was something to see, that steak flambé
Good grief, for snack tidbits, I now must pay
My mother would hate this, she went in style
And smoked her Kents with every mile
Okay, maybe I don't miss the smoking
Men in the back with cigars choking
Or maybe the flight hours need to be cut,
Whoopie, I got two pretzels, I AM in luck!

Chocolate

There is nothing I know that chocolate can't fix
Ice cream, and bars, and "bridgie" mix
White, and dark, and totally milky
We love that taste that's really silky
Give me chocolate and tell me what's wrong
Give me a Snickers while you spew your sad song
Stop looking at me as if I were loco
I want that extra dark creamy Swiss cocoa
I am fine, I can deal with all of my fears
As long as I do it with Three Musketeers

Match.com

It's not so bad, this dating scene
Some people find love, or so I've gleaned

I mean if you're lonely and want a friend
Who knows where it will end?

I know people who have dates galore
It seems every week, more and more

I wouldn't care one way or the other
If the person on screen weren't my mother

I Love You

I love you when you're sleeping
I love you when you're not
I love the way your toesies look
When your shoesies get too hot

I love your funny accents
The way your chest hairs look
I love the mess you make for me
When you want to be the cook

Do I have to draw a picture
Illustrate a big fat book
You are lucky to have my heart
You Casanova burdened crook

You are still my sweetie baby
I love you, yes I do
It will take a village harem
To finally bury you

Mourners wailing at the casket
Will all agree it's right
That you have the best of gifts
To tantalize the night

They should erect a statue
For those who serve the cause
It is a wonder to me now
Why you never got applause

Men's Noises

Men make noises, as they please
They spit, cough, snore, and wheeze
They spit in the street, they spit in the yard
Men find swallowing terribly hard

Get away from me, you pick your teeth
And let's not go clipping those ugly feet
Save these delights and don't share more
And when you "go," please close the door

Sick

Snooty receptionist or mean 'ol nurse
You won't be seeing heaven first
Smart-alecky doctor, dental clerk
You can really be total jerks
You serve the public
Or pretend you do
You'll kill us all before you're through
I'm in a wheelchair, have crutches or cane
It doesn't mean I have no brain
When the devil greets you, which I'm sure he'll do
He'll sneer and say, "May I help you?"

Sailor's Son

I fell in love with a sailor's sun;
the moon, the stars, caught my gaze
The wind was dying as I knew I was;
the deck of my soul mopped clean
When the sails catch the wind
do I then navigate my course?
Will the world be pleased with my journey?
The shining faces left behind might tell
But the sailor's son knows

Opening the Whole Foods Market

Teaming glutinous mass of humanity
Pushing towards the open doors
Fresh foods, whole foods, great foods
Like a rock concert they surged forward
Unafraid to look too eager
Unafraid to show their weaknesses
They are the American people
Confident, fat, in their smugness

Who are we, that a market opening
Brings out the upper and middle class?
Who are we that instead of culture
We harmonize to mayonnaise?
Organic, of course

Who made us so unable to even articulate
On a menu of choices for our lives?
We are corrupted by our own greed
Salivating for free morsels given
Out in tiny cups like methadone

Our world filled with unheard of choices
Yet we restrict our brains, never our palates
How sad we are, how unhappy in our democracy
We will never have real happiness
Because in a few hours we eat again

Parents and the First Day of School

Pre-K

Use the hand sanitizer on him, honey; he was with
those kids for four hours

Kindergarten

This will be great; keep the camera on him

First Grade

Do you think the other kids like the Spiderman book
bag? Get it on the video

Second Grade

Now this year, sweetie, don't hit anybody at recess;
Jim, I forgot the camera

Third Grade

Stop whining and get out of the car

Fourth Grade

Olivia is not sitting next to you; I talked to the teacher

Fifth Grade

You are going into middle school next year, no excuses on the homework, or no basketball

Sixth Grade

No decent grades, no video games, go, get out of the car

Seventh Grade

Here's the bus

Eighth Grade

No, I am not getting up; you have hands, make your
own breakfast

Ninth Grade

I know it's a new school, but remember you had to
leave the other school; get out of the car

Tenth Grade

I know you love Miss Johnson, but try not to make a
fool of yourself; she has 200 other students

Eleventh Grade

Yes the SAT's count; the afterschool prep starts today;
get out of the car

Twelfth Grade

Oh my God, honey, this is your last year; do you need
gas money? I made pancakes

Grammy

Grammy's missing we do not know
Where would she possibly have to go?
We can't find her anywhere
We need her; this isn't fair
She didn't seem to mind her last visit
Were there too many activities in it?
Maybe it was the screeching nine-year-olds
Or the baby with a snotty cold
Or the 11-year-old trying to be farty
Or the 12 other kids here for the party
She did watch "Toy Story" for the 30th time
And helped all do the jungle gym climb
She kept mumbling about Buzz and Woodie
And the baby outside without his hoodie
And then she got to see our puppy running free
Our Doberman will be bigger than you OR me
You'd think she'd never seen a dog do a pooper
She said there needed to be an inside scooper
Okay, there were a lot of games, like Chutes and
Ladders

And our six-year-old who played, got madder and
madder
I just don't understand why she left. She was making
us food
The popcorn for eight should have heightened her
mood
Oh here she is now; see, she isn't mad
We thought she left forever and that made us sad
See, she brought us popcorn for the show
She's terrific we all know
Come sit by me, and then we 'll do crafts
It's almost time for my bath

Mothers in the Hall Near the Dance

They are all there
Younger siblings doing homework,
Eating snacks under signs that forbid it
Mothers too eager for their daughters' success

Most look drained, unhappy in their giving
Are they seeking applause for the arguing?
Where are my warm-ups, my shoes, my tights?
I watch them with pity, helping the little ones

Do they hope for too much or too little?
Only one in ten have talent
Don't tell them
Don't tell them

Tastes of Childhood

Sometimes when I sit and have a terrible meal
with sticky menus and careless waiters
I think of my youth

The freshest breads from the village Boulangerie,
Artichokes dipped in butter
Veal cutlets, crisp, paper thin covering the plate,
Pommes Dauphine forced to stop floating above the
serving dish
French fries on a cold, cold, day sold on a sidewalk in
Rotterdam
Beignets from the Gare St. Lazar
And above all else, the first bite,
of a Grand Marnier Soufflé
made by loving hands at Rousello's
Twenty miles from Paris on a summer's night

Golf Buddies

We swear, we gamble
We hate women playing with us
Or in front of us
We love each other in a man way

We pee in front of each other
Sometimes in plain sight
We spit and talk about the Masters
Tiger won't be back

We love our time on Thursdays
We guard it like gold
We never miss our tee time
"You should never give up that putter"

Women Golfers

We play faster than men
We love this game
Cheaper than therapy
We talk kids, friends, and men

We never miss our tee times
And pray we will grow old together
WE do not pee in the woods
Many clubs treat us badly

We have played Scotland together
It intimidates the men
We do not talk of it
"We will give you that putt"

Masters Week

Green vestments embroidered with pine straw
Altar boys prepare the host
Transubstantiation is the back nine
Sunday, you will see the face of God

Release on ground, smooth as glass
Do not divulge your prayers
You have confessed your thoughts
Now execute your tortured soul

The inquisition trial begun
In pastels instead of black
The gallery waits and watches
Your agony on the rack begins

If you have shown your will
Let His will be done,
the shining forgiveness
Ends with a Green Jacket

21

Cell Phone

Cell phone in my face
Nature robbing disgrace
I don't want to hear you talk
While I do my quiet walk

Get that phone away; I hate your voice
But I can see I have no choice
This woman just went on speaker phone
Her undercover stupid is now blown

Another one, while I buy food,
You are so very, very, rude
Do I care how he "talked" to you?
In my opinion you should be "through"

Look at that one, texting in her car
Does she need to do that? It's not that far
Oh yes, can you see me raving?
If one life I can be saving

Reality Shows

Tramps, drunks, disgusting folk
Seriously, this must be a joke
Have you had enough of this I ask
New Jersey youth having a blast

Have we fallen, a civilization of total lead
The body is putrid, rotting at its head

Marriage

Kiss me quick and I'll pretend
I do not know how this will end
There will be foreplay for five and a half seconds
And the crow will fly south as the landscape beckons

You are so bored and I am as well
Oh, did I fake an orgasm, can you tell?
You are the closest thing I know to a rock
Must you continue to wear your socks?

Oh, this is almost done; I know for a fact
Halftime is over; I can relax

New Moon

I saw your new moon
It promised us a future
A tiny sliver

I saw your half moon
I thought we had a good life
Divorce eclipsed

I saw my full moon
Old age works
No more plans, just joy

Horse People

Horse people
Women with iron thighs
Men with Rolex wallets
Adore their life
Our horses live well

Showers, spa, massage
Perfumed trainers:
Bid for each year
Palm Beach, Aiken winters
Chicago, Long Island, left behind

Trailors, money well spent
Trust funds buy gas
See our need to be just folks
Our Bentleys smell like manure
We are common, like you

Heaven

Sin could be pride, or overeating
Or being vain, or interceding
in things that don't apply to you
Does God even have a clue?

We are so bad and want to be good
I want to be like I know that I should
So is heaven a bureaucratic mess?
You and I can only guess

We will never know, until we go
And you may not, but I will know

The Drink

They used to take the pledge, near the Blarney Stone
Wisdom to say those words; seldom quickly known
The door will open and you know in a minute
How his mood will turn, with you trapped in it

You begin to think it's you who's wrong
YOU make huge mistakes is his constant song
You cooked; you didn't; why can't you get it right
He rants and screams at you, through each dark,
night

And when you've had enough and finally try to go
He falls with pain in abject fear; he says he really
knows
How to fix the trouble, he will never drink another
day
And all you want is to trust, and all you do is pray

Life is a Banquet

Life is a banquet, that much is true
I am eating supersized foods to get over you
Bacon and cheese and big double shakes
Make your and my life seem less like a fake

My elegant prince, I believed in your style
I would have killed things, I was so beguiled
What happened to me, was it all a strange notion
That your incredible pheromones kicked into motion?

Now food does it for me, I love those eclairs
I am so sorry, I'm too fat for those stairs
A girl can rely on doughnuts and bagels
Instead of the women I know you finagle

Have fun in your life; I'm done with the sex
Unless we do it at Casa Tex Mex

Halloween

Smells of cupcakes, candy, sweets
Smells of children's hallowed treats
Grammy's here to play with the tots
She was in bed and likes sex a lot

Any opportunity to get on her back
Her favorite place is in the sack
She reads to her grandson and studies his face
Please don't tell Mommy Grammy's disgrace

She sighs and she reads *Green Eggs and Ham*
She thinks more like Popeye, "I am what I am"
Someday reading will be my only activity
Thank God for Viagra and heightened longevity

Cockroaches

Cockroaches send me to a living hell
I hate them especially where I dwell

Spray the walls and then get them out of my head
I once had three of them in my bed

What is it about them that's worse
Than snakes, or rats, or the curse

Make them leave, I hate the sight
I know they're out there in the night

The Dance

County Fair starts
Chores done,
twilight will entice
Neighbors joining them

Fifty years of work
Parents left them the farm life
They loved to dance

True high school sweethearts
Jitter bug, bop, Band Stand hopes
Dick Clark meant to call

Their sweet dance went on
In the day or in moonlight
Their dance is forever

Infidelity

It isn't the same if you see women while hidden
Then you never have to feel guilt ridden
You have honor, style, with a magnificent carriage
They unfortunately have a burden called marriage

Manet

Woman at the window sees the parade
Monet, Degas, Seurat all pass below
Manet Master was the first to blur lines
Color seamed into blobs transformed by distance
We know they stole from his genius
Later Van Gogh, Cassat, Lautrec owed him
Did he envy them? Did he care at all?
I think not because he stole as well
Velasquez, Reubens, Titian, all preceded him
Master thieves, but what jewels to steal

Hubcaps

Mustang earrings
Camaro bracelets
Nothing too good for my girl
True love

Motorcycle School

I flunked out of motorcycle school
I felt like such a big fat fool
All the others knew more than I
About the right position to fall and die

It did occur to me, mid-course
That I don't even know how to ride a horse
And now I'm catapulting myself and body
When I should be home with a rum and toddy

I made it till noon, and we all agreed
That maybe this activity wasn't me
The things my legs like to entwine
Don't have wheels, but are sublime

I'm sorry I can't stay with you
You may or may not be really blue
You'll never know I loved you enough
To try to learn to shift that clutch

Frenchman's Liver

Which door will he choose
Me, the devoted one, or booze

He is remember, "multi-brainie"
And the sex used to be "insanie"

I remember we played and I used to quiver
Now he whines like a Frenchman's liver

New Baby

Light as a feather
Entranced by those hands
They are my hands

Look at those eyes
Daddy's eyes
See the little feet
I know those little feet

I am immortal

www.ingramcontent.com/pod-product-compliance
Lightning Source LLC
Chambersburg PA
CBHW071748020426
42331CB00008B/2228